Mango Tree

Valerie Morton

Indigo Dreams Publishing

First Edition: Mango Tree
First published in Great Britain in 2013 by:
Indigo Dreams Publishing
132 Hinckley Road
Stoney Stanton
Leics
LE9 4LN

www.indigodreams.co.uk

Valerie Morton has asserted her right under the Copyright, Designs and Patents Act 1988 to be identified as the author of this work.

ISBN 978-1-909357-16-7

British Library Cataloguing in Publication Data. A CIP record for this book can be obtained from the British Library.

Designed and typeset in Palatino Linotype by Indigo Dreams.
Cover design by Karen Dennison and Ronnie Goodyer. Original photograph at Aurangabad by Eleanor Curzon.

Printed and bound in Great Britain by Imprint Academic, Exeter.

Papers used by Indigo Dreams are recyclable products made from wood grown in sustainable forests following the guidance of the Forest Stewardship Council.

For Bish

Acknowledgements

My thanks go to the Open University which provided the opportunity for me to begin this sequence and to my tutor Joel Stickley, to Bill Greenwell for teaching me about 'unnecessary words' and much more on his Exeter University Poetry Clinics and to all my friends in the Poetry Pond for their unfailing encouragement and support. A different version of Aerogramme first appeared in the *Poole Writers Circle anthology, 2009*.

Special thanks to Dawn and Ronnie at Indigo Dreams Publishing for allowing the poems to find a resting place – thank you so much.

CONTENTS

Mango Tree

You gave me India

spread it out before me
in the clashing colours of sarees
drying on the banks of the Ganges –
a chaotic palette of lights
and darks – a palette
that renews itself each morning
out of noise and disarray,
blistering heat and boisterous rain –

a palette that turns cities pink, temples gold,
and throws shadows longer than the night.

At Sea

More often now the sea flirts
with my toes, pulls me back
into the front seat of that Hillman Minx,
your warm hand on my thigh.

In the half light, we outrun
our shoes, let the incoming tide
tease our feet while our hands fiercely
seek the newness of each other

until the first seagull calls
and a muezzin cries from his minaret
on the other side of an ocean,
four thousand miles away.

Going Away

I spend my last night in the box room
listening to mother's unspoken questions.

Her open door tempts me
to spill my fears on her bed.

But if I do I may never leave,
never travel to that uncharted world of you;

never rise above a dirty January sky
and watch the familiar lights of London

switch themselves off, leaving me
suspended – never see the Cedars of Lebanon

sparkle in the sunrise or wonder
at the mountains and glaciers of the Hindu Kush –

never risk that lump in the throat
when we cross frontier after frontier,

drawing me closer to you.

Arrival

You are talking to someone
on the other side of glass. I look down
at my sensible shoes, out of place

among gold and silver
chappals peeping from under
bright sarees that sweep the floor.

In a moment you'll turn
and I am strangely shy.

New Delhi

The waking city bursts into a circus
daring acrobats on a river of bicycles.

A single scooter holds a whole family, clinging
like coral plants, chunnis waving in colours

too bright to imagine. We brush past bullock carts
that trundle as if history has forgotten them.

Close your eyes – your voice is gentle,
but limbless beggars are already remembered.

We slow only for cows chewing on garbage
as if the middle of the road was a lush meadow

half a world away. You speak names:
The Red Fort, India Gate, Connaught Place

but in the taxi I sit trim as an English lawn
while horns give way to a tree-lined road.

There are dhobis ironing in the shade and a man
leading a bear with a ring through its nose.

I try to tell you, but you are talking to the driver
in a language I can't understand.

Chandni Chowk
(Moon Market)

"You see memsahib – all India is here" –
the rickshaw wallah flashes
a paan-stained grin.

Spices sting the eyes, stay
inside the nose as we weave
round snake charmers and fortune tellers,

freewheel through tempting dishes
of chaat and jalebis. A tailor treadles –
"A suit in an hour."

Overhead, unreal Hollywood teeth
seduce from hoardings, masking
the delicate Mughal architecture

and dwarfing those omnipresent
posters of other Gods
who compete for the last word.

Waste

She lies in the gutter among rubbish, pushed
that way by hurrying feet. One small hand pokes

from under filth – a perfect hand with finger nails,
a hand I want to take in mine, but you pull me away –

away from flies that feed on her.
I can't go back to cover her, to protect her

nakedness from casual glances.
You say there's no room for sentiment

and I don't know you – a Pied Piper
who leads me through a gaudy market,

where gold flashes like a jester's teeth.

Disconnected

I wander through a day of strange sounds
locked out by my own voice.

Relatives come, curious about the woman
who's crashed into their lives.

Hindi voices rise, then lower as I pass.

I stray outside to the letter box,
hoping to find that familiar aerogramme.

I trace my fingers over English names
in the telephone directory

for any flimsy connection.

Padmasana

It's the way you sit
that betrays you
even in
your Savile Row suit
your tie knotted
to perfection:

lotus-legged
the way I never could.

As if
that small act
elevates you
and holds me
spellbound
like the white

vapour wisps
from your pipe.

padmāsana (Sanskrit) is a cross-legged sitting posture originating in
meditative practices of ancient India in which the feet are placed on the
opposing thighs. It is an established posture, commonly used for
meditation.

Chowkidar

After a steamy, sleepless night
I watch him from the balcony,
an old man bent
under a heavy shawl.

Until now he's been the tap tap
of his stick, the puff
of his whistle;
the unexpected comfort
of knowing he's there.

He doesn't look up,
but fades into the morning
calling
Subha kucha thikka hai
"All is well."

The Himalayas

Going Up

Butterflies hatch in my stomach.
The car groans and we climb past names
carved into the rocks:

Bhimtal, Nainital – havens from summers
on the plains. We twist and turn at impossible
angles allowing valleys to unwrap themselves.

I clutch your hand, dizzy and speechless
at the sheer drop on my left. Higher until
it begins to snow; a slow deepening

that closes the eyes of the ground.
We rise into cloud; our Sikh driver mutters
a prayer, touches the charm on his windscreen

and the car shudders to a stop. Muffled voices
float through white. But for a moment we stand
breathless – fluffed together – light as the air.

Morning

The smell of wood smoke, the heat
of a log fire – I've ceased wondering
how they do it without waking us.

It's stopped snowing. From our veranda
I watch the lake blink in sunlight,
disturbed only by the oars of a lone boat

leaving from the temple on the water's edge.
I feel the warmth of your breath meeting cold air,
hear you whisper *Everest* and in the distance

the shape I wish had never been conquered.
Man seems small – a dot on the bank
where the rower ties his boat.

Snow slides from the eaves. We look up
at a row of big eyes, hear the screeching
of rhesus monkeys waiting to snatch our breakfast.

Descent

The car nudges its way
through a rainbow of Holi colour
as children press *gulal* faces

on the glass and we take with us
the green, yellow and magenta
handprints of our friends

back to the plains, curling
downhill, away from snow
towards the slowly advancing heat.

But this is India – determined
to capture us with a rockfall –
a blocked road teeming

with young women in red and
yellow mirrored sarees
shifting stones, carrying

heavy baskets on their heads
as though each one
was no more than a feather.

We perch in the shade
by a stream of melting snow,
its refreshing water

accompanying gifts of
chapatis and vegetables.
I rest my head against you

and watch our driver unwind
his turban, shake loose
endless curls that tumble

like water over rocks.

Agra

Outbound

In the half light
we pull away from Delhi,
pick up speed
through vast plains dotted
with men squatting
at morning ablutions

unashamedly waving
at our faces framed
in the window
of the Taj Express, steaming
in her best navy and cream

across the backside of India
that leaves its dung to dry
in the fast-rising sun.
We sit, oddly detached
in first class
air-conditioned luxury,

sipping tea
from Royal Doulton china.

The Taj Mahal

Ever the sceptic, I fear
our meeting will disappoint.
But as I walk through the arch
that February morning

it feels as if the breath
is squeezed from my lungs,
leaving me gasping like a baby
exposed to light for the first time.

Return

We are back in the dimly
lit carriage, sipping tea.

The darkness suits our mood –
different now – changed

by something shared
yet not completely understood.

Mango Tree

You take me to your village –
to the mango grove where
you'd met the cobra.

You show me the place
where it slept in the heat
before unwinding

to a child's height
and rocking
from side to side

in fury or confusion –
you didn't stay long enough
to find out. I feel you hesitate

on the edge of the long grass
and my own feet refuse
to move, in case it's been waiting

all those years,
to make certain
you and I could never be.

Mango

You peel back

the smooth skin, feed me
        slippery yellow flesh.

I hold its sweetness
        on my tongue,

against my palate;
        feel its flavour

explode as cool juices
        spill down my cleavage.

*For weeks we've felt restless in the heat, a prickly heat relieved only
partially by whirring fans. This evening is hotter than ever and we sit
gloomy, despondent with inertia, playing Beethoven's Ninth
Symphony on an old Grundig tape recorder when the sky darkens and
the smell of the first huge drops of rain reaches our nostrils. Within
seconds it's a deluge, striking the dry and cracked earth and pounding
on the verandah like a rescuer arriving after a long siege. It rises and
falls in tune with the music as we stand outside for twenty minutes,
soaking ourselves in new life. And then the sun comes out.*

Music of the Monsoon

The sky uncorks itself, spilling
a mass of sunbaked sewage
in a gurgling overture.

Trees turn green, verandas drip
as a million frogs heave up
to a rousing symphony.

Cicadas pulse stiff muscles,
emerge from cracked mud
to click their courtship song.

And as if released through
a safety net, a million lacewings
serenade the night.

By dawn, the sky is squeezed dry:
buildings etched stark white
against unbroken blue

in perfect harmony.

On the Road

We slow down for a man thrashing
a dead horse; try to avoid his overturned cart,

its cargo of mangos rolling across the wet road
in sun-ripe reds, greens and yellows.

The wasted carcass no longer feels the whip;
open eyes stare at nothing. And all the time

the rain streams like tears
down the man's weather-wracked face

while laughing children rush about,
filling their pockets and skirts,

dodging cars that spurt past and squash
what's left for the rain to wash away.

Vultures start dropping from the sky.

Dusk turns to dark quickly as we reach the outskirts of New Delhi,
our headlights the only light on the road. Then suddenly ahead of us I
see little flickerings as if stars are falling to earth. And before long we
are driving through an avenue of flashing lanterns flitting and flying
through the trees. You begin to give me a science lesson, but I ask you
to hush – I want to wonder at the magic of the moment I first watch
fireflies dance.

Fireflies

Dusk ends suddenly here; no slow slide
through evening shadows towards the dark.
Kerosene lamps glow on the verges

and from dung fires a constant brew
of thick muddy tea, milk and sugar mingles
with the heady scent of nocturnal blooming

jasmine. And as midnight creeps closer
there's no need for *tygers burning bright*,
or the amber eyes of the panther.

Trees begin to flash until they explode
with a flaming ardour, as if signalling
the premature birth of *Diwali*.

The Queue

I stand at the tail end of a queue
at the post office – the only blue

in a line of sparkling white,
of smiles and *namastes*.

Little boys squat to clean my shoes;
little girls touch my tights, giggle

then run away. No-one comes behind
but still I stand and wait

while the smiles grow longer and wider
and I feel my feet take root

in the dry soil.

Wearing a Sari

A silent waterfall of silk
paintbrushes the floor –
cascading
like a trellis of roses

making its own breeze
from lightly whispered secrets
that hover
on an invisible thread

Hindu Wedding

Night of white horses
Seven steps around the fire
The scent of jasmine

In this crazy night
We stay close to each other
Afraid to let go

Going Home

Goodbye is strange – no words –
just my eyes glued to yours
over a sea of well-wishers.

I've only stroked the skin of India
but she has opened her folded hands
to me and I'm not ready

to leave the rains that quench the dust
or the peacocks that strut
their ritual dance in fast-falling dusk.

Instead I take with me the scent
of dung fires, sandalwood
and rose-red cities in a suitcase

heavy with departure. I put on
my homebound face and shrink
into the bustle of Palam Airport

clutching a ticket that says *Return*.
I know it will be raining in London.

Post-Script

Aerogramme

Perhaps you've seen me
in the market, stirred by the sway
of a skirt, the turn of a head.

Maybe you've scanned the stars
as you stretch towards
an empty pillow, smooth

from my absence. Or read
my name in every constellation,
following my body's curves

across the contours
of the moon. Did you taste
the salt of me as you licked

the wafer thin paper? I hold it
up to the light, trace a finger
over the dimples where you pressed

with your pen. As long
as its blueness lies whole
on my palm I am still with you.

Indigo Dreams Publishing
132, Hinckley Road
Stoney Stanton
Leicestershire
LE9 4LN
www.indigodreams.co.uk